FAR FLUNG FRAGMENTS

Piers Blaikie

Contents

Dedication

I dedicate 'Far Flung Fragments to a group of writers of poetry and short fiction who get together every Thursday in Norwich and are appropriately called The Thursday Morning Writers. Over the last twenty years, much of my creative writing has been nurtured by this group. Since its inception, it has published seven anthologies and helped to stimulate its members to write many individual works of their own. I feel forever obliged to this group for their friendly, constructive and stimulating company. Also, I dedicate this book to Tom Corbett, who started the group and has inspired it over the years.

Acknowledgements

Several pieces in this collection appeared in anthologies written by a group of authors, the Thursday Morning Writers and published by Gatehouse Press.

The author would also like to acknowledge the excellent service of Savvy Book Marketing who transformed an original manuscript into publishable form with efficiency and speed.

About the Author

Piers Blaikie is a retired professor from the School of International Development at the University of East Anglia, Norwich. His work often involved travelling to and living in remote parts of Africa, Asia and the New World. He found his forty-year career there profoundly fulfilling from a political and academic aspect, but also a gallop of the imagination across deserts, mountains, teeming cities, wild forests (with low hanging branches!), and unforgettable people. Much of the anthology drew its inspiration from this experience. While a few fragments have autobiographical origins, most do not draw upon them specifically.

April 24th 2015

Suddenly street dogs burst out barking. Rooks scatter from pavements to perch uncertainly on telegraph wires. A few feel the ground tremble. Some sigh and go back to sleep. It is four in the morning. The Pathak family, huddled on one huge string bed, hardly stir.

Another two hours go by uneventful and by six o'clock, the city is choked with the daily rush to work. People flowing, porters labouring, scooters dodging, kids laughing, mothers clucking and taxis, packed with people and bulging with baggage, barging their way through. Susma and Indra hold their mother's hand on their way to school. It's an ordinary morning like any other. The city comes alive for another day.

A week passes.

The afternoon is in full flow when suddenly, just before three o'clock, for no apparent reason, two riders suddenly fall off their bikes by the side of the road, close to where mother Pathak and her children are walking. Pedestrians stumble, cars screech to a halt, and people gather in ragged lines in the middle of the street. It is a screaming look for loved ones lost in the crowd as the ground shudders. Temples sway and start to collapse, shedding tiles and bricks in a crumbling heap, blanketed in clouds of dust. Cracks appear in walls and within seconds, concrete buildings start to gape. Sizeable lumps tumble into the streets below. The shaking stops, but the harrowing screams, rushing feet, and falling masonry continue.

Buildings groan and, almost as an afterthought, decide to collapse, falling debris hitting street pavements. A huge piece of concrete hurtles towards mother Pathak and her two children returning from school. There is an ear-splitting, blinding flash that she can never describe but will always be engraved in her memory. In a split second, the realization hits her that her son, Indra, is no longer holding her hand. Bewildered, she staggers to her feet and starts looking for him. Her daughter, Susma follows, gripping her sari and stumbling after her. They search, dithering, wailing, looking, and hoping. But Indra is nowhere to be found. Nowhere at all.

After a while, she begins to think clearly and seeks her husband to help find Indra. Their house is only three streets away. Perhaps they can find him together, but first, she has to find her husband. Then, by unlikely good fortune, she spots him helping other men, helping people out of the debris. They run towards each other and breathlessly embrace. She gasps her story to him and they set off together with Susma to find their son.

The streets between their house and where she lost Indra are lined with old timber-framed brick buildings. Most of them have heaved themselves into precarious positions or collapsed completely, but some are still shedding occasional tiles into the street around the Pathak parents who are dashing everywhere in search of their son. They are heedless of any danger now as they approach the street where Indra disappeared. A bleak scene of the milling crowd, dust and ruinous buildings meet them. She shows her husband where she lost him, but neither of them can find any evidence of him dead or alive. They wander, searching, but after some hours, her husband shakes his head and starts wailing quietly. They return home to find that it is probably unsafe to enter, but he decides to go in any way to retrieve their most essential possessions. Susma has not eaten since the morning. He throws food, bedding and kitchen utensils out of the window while his wife catches them while standing in the street. Now what? Their misfortune has just begun.

They return again to the place where Indra disappeared. The crowd has dispersed and the street has more or less cleared. Yet, there is no sign of Indra, of course. They return home and stop at a tea shop that has managed to open up against all the odds. They sit in silence on a bench in the street, sip tea and listen to the local radio. The news is all about the earthquake. Early estimates of some thousands killed in the capital, but one hundred kilometres further west casualties are much higher. Not only the earthquake itself but landslides, mudflows and avalanches have wiped off some villages completely. They look at each other with dread.

They know fully well that their family house is there and most of their relatives live there. But they shake their heads and say nothing. After half an hour, they get up and walk home, all hope in their hearts vanquished.

Only to find Indra sitting with a stranger on the pavement outside their house.

April in Paris

It was April 1963 in Paris. I was sharing a bunk with an Algerian man. We were both on shift work in a factory in the suburbs of Paris and were sleeping in a grimy hostel. We had shared a bunk a number of times before and, over time, found him a friendly and equable bed companion. Workers were constantly blundering into the hostel at the end of their shifts and collapsing exhausted into any empty or part unoccupied bunk.

One night, about three o'clock in the morning, I was awakened by my bunk companion lying huddled by my side. He was pleading, praying and begging in Algerian Arabic dialect. I distinguished the words "Allahu Akbar", so I assumed it was a prayer. It sounded such a desperate request that I felt I was overhearing a prayer of great personal importance and one I should not hear at all. After a minute or so, I murmured:

"Alors, il y a une probleme, ou quoi?"

"I want a cigarette. I just want one. Just one."

"What! Is that all?"

I couldn't see his expression in the dark, but I could guess it. I knew any helpful reply would require inspiration – or even better, a cigarette, but he knew I did not smoke and couldn't give him one. I might miss my chance of saying something transforming to him as well as myself. What a

chance! But no amount of thinking could make it any better.
So, back to sleep .

The Magic Hum

There is a girl who hums a tune.
Birds stop their song and listen.
So sweet, flowers burst and bloom.
Open out, gleam and glisten.

People turn heads and cock an ear,
Babies stop their crying, start to dream.
It calms their worry, soothes their fears,
They hear its gentle theme.

Then one day, as she hums along,
Down the pathway to her school,
A man comes, shady, plainly wrong,
Slick, slimy, smiling, cool.

"I heard that tune you hummed so well.
Could it be you'd let me write it down?
We'll share it, market it, and it'll sell."
She answers with a frown.

She turns away, hums her tuneful spell,
We do not know what might have come
For her to sing to the world, then sell,
And forever spoil that magic hum.

Karoo

A wheezing jeep bucks like a boat,
Heaving over a sea of grass towards a reef.
A huddle of lumbering boulders
Set in sweeping shadows of the Karoo.
It will rain soon, black-lipped clouds
Stitched with lightning, booming
Coming soon.

We disembark, clamber over the rise.
Find the place where the San once were.
Here before black warriors from the North,
With short stabbing spears.
Here before white farmers from the South
With sharp spitting guns.
The San shot at, driven away, shot out,
The first vermin of the veldt.

We come now to hear their singing stones,
Notes knocked from rounded rocks,
To see their etchings of beasts and spirits,
Their dreams from the edge of their world.

The lion stands still upon the stone,
Whiskers bristling with intent.

A deer bounds away in terror
Its neck stretched towards safety.
An ostrich flaps wildly for its life.
They've almost made it off the stone.
But the lion stands still,
Bristling, watching
Over centuries, etched in stone.

Black spots of thunderous rain spatter the stones.
The storm is upon us.
Downwind the last fugitive sunshine.
Chases shadows, amber, silver, mercury and lead.
Turn around, see the world bruised dark
Closing a curtain across space and time.

Borderlines

The trading barque lay in the mouth of the Hooghly River, heaving slowly with the swell and the rigging rhythmically slatting against the sails. The sea was brown, and the distant horizon was smudged with mud banks. It was hot, and only a breath of wind offered some respite from the heat every now and then. The flood tide that would take the ship up to Calcutta port was to hit them in a few hours, but for now, they were almost stationary. George Logan stepped out of the cabin in search of cooler air only to draw into his lungs the same fetid air he had sought to escape in the cabin. After a voyage of nine weeks, he wanted to start negotiating the price of possible return cargoes; cotton, silk, indigo, saltpetre, or tea. As manager and co-owner of the trading Company, he had negotiated cargoes with the Company before.

Everyone aboard – George, his assistant James Montieth, three missionaries, a medical doctor, the captain and the crew all suffered strange, contradictory feelings – weariness and, at the same time, impatience. After ten weeks of sailing, everyone wanted to have their feet on dry land, to relax, eat fresh food and go about their usual routines. George withdrew to a shady spot by the taffrail and stared moodily at sea.

Then all of a sudden, he saw the flotsam, a disintegrating raft of half-burnt branches and twigs with other material adhering to it. As the ship sailed slowly past, George caught sight of a human skull with flesh sticking to the nose and jaw, half-burnt and shredded in long tails of skin. Gobbets of entrails gently wafted in the seawater, lapping the raft. He was horrified beyond any violent shudder of disgust, but horror has its own fascination, so he continued to look until the ship slid past the sight, and it slowly disappeared around the aft. He returned to his cabin and retched.

Fourteen hours later, at high tide, it was ten minutes past noon on September 9th. The sailing ship, Artemis, docked at one of the Company's wharves. George and Monteith went to the Council Chambers to register their arrival and incoming cargo and to set up meetings to discuss the purchase of possible exports to the United Kingdom.

The next day, George was travelling by carriage from the Company offices to the Auckland Hotel in the city. Most of the route was lined with imperial buildings and reassured him that he was still within the oasis of a civilized society. But even here, he could not help noticing the signs of decay on buildings, bridges and monuments almost as soon as they were constructed. Some side streets led away from the spacious and orderly to a dark and seething India. His eye noticed at least six small heaps of filthy clothing lying by the side of the road - corpses. After seeing them, his mind was forced to think about them. Even a single abandoned corpse was unusual in a busy thoroughfare of the biggest city in India. He wondered why no one had claimed them to give funeral rites. Then, without warning, the carriage veered across the broad street and lurched down a dark side street. George immediately shouted at the tongawallah, who replied, "Short-cut, short-cut, Sahib!" George started to object, but his voice was now inaudible above the clatter of horses' hooves. Soon the carriage was moving along a tree-lined road, and he noticed vague shapes of people squatting and huddled around small fires lit on the verges. They stretched far as his eye could see into the distance. Many hundreds of families seemed to be living in the open. The air was heavy with the smell of burning cow dung and ordure while the neighbourhood was in almost complete silence, except for an occasional sound of a child crying in the distance. George peered out from the carriage, fearful of having to contemplate any further evidence of moral darkness or the possibility of witnessing death in large numbers.

The carriage suddenly came to a slithering halt. George looked out and saw a man in the middle of the road, walking slowly towards the carriage. He was completely naked, his genitals lolling gently with each step. One of his legs was severed above the knee, and he hobbled with the aid of a crutch. His body was smeared in ash, giving him a ghostly look. He was chanting a prayer while his eyes were set vaguely in front of him. Suddenly, he saw George, and what happened next, George would remember for the rest of his days. The man stopped, looked at him directly and then he smirked - a lop-sided toothless smirk. It was a smirk of shared understanding of duplicity and of shared secrets that slowly masked the face of the man. He knew and knew that George knew. George was slowly consumed by a wave of self-blame, its origins beneath his conscious reasoning. Where it came from and what sins had created it; he had no idea. He slumped back into the carriage, gasping, scouring his conscience to no avail. George emerged shaken and sweating from the carriage at the Auckland Hotel. At least, the hotel commanded a familiar view of imperial buildings, and he could relax in civilized surroundings. Servants bustled to carry his luggage into the huge hotel hall. He bathed and settled down to write a letter home.

Excerpts from a letter written by George Logan to his family in Melrose, Scotland:

September 14th, 1849
My dear brother,

I again address you from the shores of India, where it seems my lot to spend much of my life, and possibly maybe the land where my frail body may be committed to its parent dust.

The Doctor, my assistant and I have all been well, but there has been a good deal of sickness on board the ship, and a fine young man has died of cholera. I hope we shall be able to leave Calcutta within a matter of weeks. We are looking forward to being able to return to London by the middle of December. We do not intend to visit any intermediate port between Calcutta and London, but I hear that the Company wishes to have transported an elephant passenger for a client, who, I understand, means to cage these creatures and charge people for the sight of this and other animals of the wild. It is a most unusual cargo, and one that I deem will cause us some difficulty if we are to deliver it alive. It should be much given to drinking large volumes of water, for want of which we may be obliged to visit the Cape of St. Helena.

It was just two years to a day from my last arrival at Calcutta – a period short in itself and still shorter to me when looking back – in truth; it did not seem six months. The poor blinded and degraded natives die literally like sheep in a severe winter, with scarcely a neighbour to exhibit the least sympathy for their sufferings or give them a drink of water. They have hardly any thought for tomorrow, and as to a future state, they have hardly any ideas upon the subject. Their methods of disposal of their relatives and loved ones at burial are without care and are a demonstration that lacks respect for the departed soul. They cover the corpse with firewood, set it alight and put the whole raft in the river to float away. The fire is usually extinguished without consuming the corpse either due to an insufficiency of wood or due to the extinguishing of the fire by river water. This shameful practice shows an indecent disregard for the dignity of those who passed away as well as for the living who will take away an odious last glimpse of their loved ones.

I hope on my arrival at the offices of the Company; I shall find letters from you. I have full confidence that you and your family will maintain the grave of my dear Mary and nourish her sweet memory with flowers. I love you all with unabated affection, and the hope that you cherish the same thoughts towards me is gratifying to my heart. My very best wishes to your dear partner and children and to other members of your family around you.

I remain,
Your brother,
George

Two days later, George was invited to a dinner by a senior Company official with whom he had done business on a previous trip. His carriage clatters up to the edifice of the Writers Building. He peers out to find couples strolling past its imposing frontage in the evening cool. Assured men in light tunics and extravagant ruffs with their women in sweeping dresses and fashionable hats chat easily as they stroll in the evening air before turning in for dinner. He pays off the carriage at some distance from the club building and walks to its magisterial entrance. The central hall was crowded with guests. Brays of laughter from men drinking their fourth glass of claret and squeaks of amusement from ladies punctuated the uproar. Liveried servants navigated neatly between guests to replenish empty glasses. Such reckless hilarity was not to George's liking. However, upon being offered a large glass of claret himself, he abandons his principles, accepts it, takes a deep draft and peers around the hall. Banks of candles along the walls were lit, and glittering chandeliers twinkled below the vaulted ceiling. However, there was no sign of the senior Company official who had invited him to the occasion. He was still looking around for the senior officer when he noticed a family group with whom he had stayed two years before. The man, James Carslaw, caught his eye, who was shouting a friendly welcome that was more or less inaudible above the noise. He waved him over and resumed talking to his family. The younger woman at his side strayed from their conversation and spotted George. She smiled at him, although he was certain he had not met her before on his last visit. She whispered something to James and nodded in George's direction, after which they both beckoned him over to join the group. After exchanging welcomes with James and his wife, Rebecca, George was introduced to the new woman.

'George, I believe you have not met my younger sister, Sarah. She has recently joined us here in Calcutta. Sarah, this is George Logan. He is a ship owner and trades with the Company. We have enjoyed his company at our residence on a number of previous visits.'

After further customary pleasantries, George felt he should tell them that his wife had died the previous year. He could just manage to bear the family's condolences and was happy for him to move the conversation onto his voyage to Calcutta.

'We had an agreeable journey and by His Grace, we arrived safely two days previously. But, I must tell you, upon my journey from the Auckland hotel to the Company's offices just this past few days I was, may I say, shocked by what I saw.'

A distancing look quickly appeared on the faces of the group. This was not the sort of subject one brings up at a party such as this. However, George did not notice.

'I saw corpses in the street abandoned without burial or burning, without any care or ceremony. I saw many poor natives without shelter, clearly in direst need, maybe some even starving. Vagrants, I presume. I ……'

James Carslaw drew a deep breath and looked down at the table. 'Of course since you have scarcely arrived, you will not know that in the past year we have been visited by pestilence. Smallpox has struck the city. A thousand or more have died, not only in the Company's barracks, but here too amongst whole families, even among our friends. It is likely that the natives you saw lying dead in the street were victims too. Now - shall we move onto more agreeable matters?'

Sarah cut into the conversation without so much as a glance at James.

'I can see you are an observant man, Mr Logan. The "vagrants"' (spoken with heavy irony) are, in fact, starving. They are without food, and they will die, not in hundreds from smallpox as my dear brother has explained, but in many thousands. One of the main reasons is…'

'Sarah! That is enough. You are not six months arrived from England and have yet to comprehend the complexities of our life here.'

Sarah again looked at George and continued to speak directly to him as if her brother had not spoken.

'They die in their thousands here in Bengal because landlords here trade opium with the "Honourable" East India Company. Opium is fifty times more profitable than rice. The landlord takes the profit, of course, but the land can no longer be cultivated by the labourers to grow the rice on which they rely on for food. Hence, they starve. Then…'

'That, Sarah, is enough', and this time James grabbed Sarah's arm and gave it a hard squeeze, but she kept on looking at George with a faint smile.

The sound of a gong, struck by a huge dignified Indian servant dressed in the magnificent garb of a nabob, gave the signal for dinner. Cheers from some of the men and the boisterous chatter of the crowd altered as guests started moving to the dining hall. George succumbed to another glass of claret and was guided to a seat on one of the six tables set in the hall. He found himself sitting next to one of the Company's Writers, and judging by his supercilious manner and accent; he seemed to be with aristocratic connections. He was happy to be sitting nearly opposite Sarah, who acknowledged him again with a smile.

'So, sir, I understand you are trading with the Company?' said the Writer languidly.

'I am, indeed. At the present, we are negotiating terms for export of jute, cotton and maybe silk, if we can negotiate a suitable price. Silk.....'

'Ah, silk, sir. May I congratulate you, sir, on such a choice of trade? Now, China....'

Suddenly a woman's voice from across the table, almost shouting in order to be heard above the clamour, cut in.

'Yes, you may congratulate him, sir, on being a partner in an unjust and foul trade. The only reason that we, the "Honourable" East India Company can afford to balance trade with China is to forcibly sell opium to them, grown by factories in India and sold to traders for silver. You, Mr. Logan, are part of that trade,' Sarah was still smiling at him.

George had heard about the trade and the war that followed from reports in the United Kingdom but had always considered it as not his business. After all, he did not trade opium. Before he had time to reply, the Writer put down his fork and addressed Sarah, rather than George,

'Madam', then speaking very slowly as if explaining to a child, 'We are a trading company. We trade with China and many other countries, and for this trade to be successfully carried out, there are rules - universal rules which must be universally obeyed by all who partake in exchanges all over the world. The issue of opium is not our business. After all, do we have the right to pass moral judgments upon the internal ethics of those countries with whom we do business? I think not. Do I make myself clear?'

'I can see, sir, this is turning into a lecture. Remember. Such a moral issue elicited Mr Gladstone no less, to call this trade "infamous and unjust".'

'And also, madam, if I may be permitted to add, it was our Prime Minister, Lord Palmerston, who justified, or shall I say rightly justified, military action to enforce the terms of free trade, which, I may remind you, are the same for everyone. It is a matter of price and a free choice to buy and sell. And that the commodity is opium is not a matter of importance. If the client - in this case, China - is a willing buyer and our East India Company is a willing seller, it is no one's business to plead for special circumstances.' He turned away and spooned in another mouthful of beef stew. Then he resumed, now addressing George with a sardonic twist to his lips.

'Sir, if I am not mistaken, your fellow countrymen were, and, I believe, still are leading in trading opium. Mr Jardine, now departed this world some nine years ago, and Mr Matheson (now a baronet, no less, back in your Scotland) were some of the most successful traders in opium. I trust your national bent for trade will lead you to similar rewards.' He smiles again before taking another spoonful of stew.

George finds himself unable to reply. He gulps some claret and remembers the smirk of the man with an ashen face and one leg. Surely he could not have known George's business. Surely not? Maybe he saw George as a white man, any white man, and made the assumption that greed, guilt and heartlessness attended all white men. His smile was so complicit. The unease that accompanied his trading ventures once more emerges, but he manages to distance himself from any direct responsibility. After all, his business is a trade and not to take responsibility for its impact upon a society, which he does not understand and, in any case, whose misfortunes arise from a debased social and religious culture.

He had consumed more wine than he had ever done and vaguely realised that he was moving outside what was safe - the familiar sights, sounds, language and the foundations of his solid and predictable life. He was now at sea, but not as a trader in his ship crossing oceans. The dinner held no further interest for him, and he had to wait for another hour before guests started to leave.

Excerpts from Letter written by George Logan:-
September 18th, 1849
My dear brother,

Since I last wrote to you, I am happy to say our business with the Company has every prospect of turning out well. Montieth and I have managed to negotiate a cargo of cotton, tea and jute. However, I have yet to negotiate a price for the transportation of the elephant about which I wrote to you before. There is also a consignment of silk from China, but the Company is sceptical of the prices they would want to negotiate. I hear from informal sources that the silk trade and that of other commodities are now very uncertain. You probably know of the war between the Chinese and the Company, where I am given to understand, a zealous and hasty Chinese functionary destroyed a consignment of opium belonging to the Company. War is not the companion of free trade that is beneficial to all.

In the meantime, in my daily life, I move within the perimeter of an ordered society, but I continue to glimpse the world beyond. It is one with whom we trade but not admit beyond the boundaries of acceptable Christian behaviour. I have already written about the sight of a floating mass of charred remains of a corpse, bearing witness to Hindoo practices of how a departed soul is dispatched to eternity. I have more to share with you. Since my last voyage to Calcutta, many sad changes have taken place in this fatal climate – several of those who were members of the small circle I associated with rest in the graves – others who at my last visit were in good health are now apparently on the verge of departure from life. I supposed ten years in this country completely changed the lives of the European inhabitants. Is not such a consideration calculated to make men more thoughtful and attentive to their eternal welfare? But such is not their conduct -- I do believe that where there is the greatest waste of human life, there you will see the greatest indifference to eternity. In the streets, even in the broad thoroughfares, I see many corpses lying abandoned, without any evidence of last rites that may mark their departure from this world. I also bore witness to great crowds of starving men, women and children and learnt from reliable sources that many are made destitute by the Company's encouragement of cultivating opium in the fields of Bengal that used to grow paddy for the labourers. Hitherto, I'm of the view that starvation came about through lack of forethought of the poor and the greed of the rich. It now seems that the Company has given a rod to the rich and forgotten the poor who have no part to play in the negotiation of our trade. Furthermore, the Company has corrupted the rulers of China by offering them undreamt-of riches if they accept the importation of opium, thus debauching an entire nation. It was pointed out to me that I willingly trade with the Company and, therefore, have complicity in this arrangement. Still, my dear brother, I feel that any complicity is too remote for me to desist in the trade of other harmless commodities.

Your affectionate brother,
George

A week later, George was able to take up James's invitation to stay. He remembered with contentment the large rambling family bungalow with a wide verandah and a view of a fine garden and distant imperial buildings visible in the haze which surrounded the city in winter. He joined the family on many congenial evenings, talking to James's wife, Rebecca, and their children, who had grown in stature and confidence since his last visit. George was very busy. There was a continuing need to visit the Writers Building, bid for cargo and arrange for its loading and payment. He also wrangled with the owners of the elephant, which he was supposed to take to London. He was alarmed to hear that one seaman of his crew had already succumbed to smallpox. Three others had contracted venereal disease following visits to the numerous brothels in the city and treated the news as a trespass of disease and immorality from India into his civilised world.

However, evenings at the Carslaw residence provided a refuge for relaxation and discussion. On a number of evenings before dinner, Sarah visited him on the verandah of the guest's bungalow. She told him of her involvement with the establishment of schools in Calcutta for Bengali girls. She explained the diversity of different reformers. A loose and often mutually contradictory alliance of leading Bengali reformists, Christian missionaries, British philanthropists and educationalists had succeeded in setting up a number of schools in the city. Sarah talked animatedly about the achievements of this movement. These discussions continued over a few weeks, during which time George was happy to listen to her and quietly admired her sharp mobile face, which animated whatever words she spoke – with humour, frustration, disapproval and delight. He realised he was happy again for the first time since his wife's death. He quietly acknowledged to himself that unfamiliar romantic feelings had crept up on him before he could develop a rational resistance to such an impractical, even improper liaison.

A few days before he was due to sail back to London, they reached a tipping point in their conversations. Sarah was telling him about a meeting that day with the staff of the newest girls' college in the city, and she directly expressed her opposition to a Christianising evangelical basis to education. This time, she fixed him with a questioning look softened by the smile he had become so used to and so much wished to win. This time George expressed his conviction clearly, risking the warmth and companionship of their evenings spent together.

'But surely it is the missionaries who must evangelise education and bring proper Christian values to the benighted Hindus. It is clear....'

'George, please be so good as to listen. In all the times you have visited Calcutta, you have never once crossed the line to the other side with the purpose of learning about the Bengali people, about the women and children we want to help. Instead, you cower behind a missionary mantra;' she hesitated and waved her hand as she sought an English translation, 'a missionary formula by which you judge all those who do not believe in Christ as benighted, as evil and bereft of any sense of humanity. You have said so yourself. You....'

George gazed at her as she talked. He saw her sparkling brown eyes, but this time that immanent smile that usually promised so much did not appear. He was suffused with warmth for her at the precise moment of profoundly disagreeing with what he saw as her core value. He involuntarily took her hand that lay beside his. For a long moment, she allowed her hand to stay there. Then she withdrew it and laid it over his.

'No, George. Dear, dear George. This isn't possible.' She looked away from him and gently shook her head.

Five days before the planned departure of the Artemis, there was a major upset in George's trading plans. The consignment of tea for which Montieth had bid for did not arrive. Without this consignment, the profitability of the voyage would be seriously compromised. They enquired of the Writers of the Company and freelance traders about alternative cargoes. George learned with a sinking feeling that the Writer with whom he was to deal with was none other than the aristocratic Englishman he had met at the dinner some weeks before.

'Ah, Mr… er Logan. Here you are again. I understand you wish to discuss with me the possibility of purchase of some merchandise from China. Silk, or perhaps decorative pottery? I remember our discussion at dinner with your good self and that strident lady– if I may be permitted to describe her thus - sitting opposite us. I can see you have re-aligned your views on trade and ethics, then?'

George mumbled an excuse he prefered to forget and looked up at the gentleman, who was smirking at him with obvious pleasure.

'I am told that a trader from the United States of America has failed to materialise, and their cargo of silk and decorative pottery from China would be available for purchase.' George could not give an affirmative answer, and the Writer was faintly amused.

'I think you will find that there are a number of alternative traders who are only too willing to avail themselves of these purchases. I must ask you, sir, to give me a firm acceptance of my offer now, or I will withdraw it forthwith.' A faint condescending smile hovered on his face. George felt he had no alternative but to agree on a price for the goods; otherwise, he faced the possibility of serious loss.

A week later, the Artemis was being towed by a wheezing, shuffling tug down the Hooghly roads, lined with a forest of masts. The elephant bellowed its dismay at the noise and buffeted the temporary pen that had been constructed on the foredeck. The poor animal was terrified. George watched it from within the main deck saloon and asked himself what on earth he was doing, transporting a terrified native animal to a cage in a foreign country so that people could pay money to look at it. There was also the danger that there might not be sufficient water for it, and if so, it would expire. On the other hand, he told himself, this was a trading agreement between the Company and an entrepreneur in London, and it was not his business to enquire into the ethics of the transaction. He had not mentioned the last-minute changes to the type of cargo he was to take to James's household, although he knew well that the information would eventually reach them – but after he had left.

He looked up and peered through the companionway to the muddy banks of the Hooghly. 'Perhaps,' he mused, 'faith alone is not enough to keep one from sin. I have no direct responsibility for a benighted India, but, yes, I find that I am nonetheless contaminated by trading with the Company. Therefore, it is inescapable that I am playing a small part in the misfortunes of the Bengali and Chinese people.' He saw Sarah's smile and heard her powerful and precise remarks that would follow. He sighed wistfully, and then his attention turned to the large profit that his cargo would probably make him. Self-disgust and sadness settled beside the satisfaction of a lucrative trading deal.

He caught sight again of the elephant. It suddenly seemed to have accepted its strange and threatening environment and was calm and motionless. It extended its trunk towards the commotion caused by the tug towing the Artemis and the men working on the foredeck to catch their scent. George smiled. He, too, had accepted a strange and perhaps an alarming future. 'The dilemma between trade and morality is irreconcilable. I have decided I will sell my directorate and trading interests and retire to Melrose to be near my dear brother since I will be without a life companion. I will invest my capital in the new agriculture. I will lead a new life, a blameless life and a lonely life.'

Ten weeks of sailing, and he would be home.

Broken Bargain

At the edge of the forest stood an ancient tree, and under it, cradled by gnarled roots, sat a godling - or perhaps to others' eyes, a goblin, or a shrunken human perhaps. In any case, it was now hardly recognisable through hundreds of years of stroking and anointing with ghii. An old man hobbled towards the tree in the last rays of the sun and kneeled before it. His name was Sidhu. He had come to bargain.

He started by singing supplications and then made his request. He was asking for the death of the local landlord. For a paltry sum long since spent on local hooch, he had delivered his son into a five-year labour agreement with the landlord by which he was to work his bidding for a meagre handful of rice a day. Sidhu once went to intercede with the landlord but was thrown out by his hired bully. He remembered, as he was being beaten, the landlord shouting, "Get out, you filthy, polluting tribal!" His fury was stoked by his inability to do anything about it – except perhaps through prayer. He knew that he had to sacrifice something to ensure the godling would answer his prayers. He offered the sacrifice of a goat a week until his prayers were answered. Somehow he got the feeling the godling was asking him to sacrifice two goats. After wailing and muttering, he agreed to the sacrifice of two goats, struggled to his feet and walked home in the evening sun.

The next day he was woken early by a great commotion in the village. There was the police, a jeep and villagers, shouting and crowding around the police sergeant. Sidhu learned that the landlord had been murdered in the night and guessed that the Maoist guerrillas were to blame. He pottered about his home in a daze of delight. The godling had responded promptly to his prayer, and he realised that he would soon see his son. Sure enough, he arrived and ran into his father's arms.

A week passed, and Sidhu thought that he needed not sacrifice his second goat after all. On the ninth day after the bargain was reached, he celebrated the fulfilment of his prayer by drinking a bottle of the local fiery hooch. As he dozed off in front of his house, the police suddenly appeared to demand that his son should return to fulfil the agreement of indentured labour for a further five years. The contract still stood valid whether the landlord was alive or not. The policeman started to threaten him with arrest unless he delivered his son back to the landlord's estate.

Sonnet for the sub-conscious

Some memories are false, but they feed us
Others are lost and cannot be brought to mind.
And they are the ones that need us,
But not knowing where to look, we cannot find.

Never believe memories come unbidden
Selected by what conscious minds allow,
What stays beneath the waves remains hidden
Lost in nets of synapses, lost to here and now.

Are not lost memories more important by far?
We dream and dive into shadows of the deep,
But not knowing what they are,
Blindly grope for what lies in depths of sleep.

Strange marks of memory in the sand are easy to find.
What is hard is to own them and bring them to mind.

I Will Kill You

The lounge bar of the overnight ferry to Southampton was crammed with returning holidaymakers, all barging for a beer at the bar. There was very little seating, and Marcus had carefully put his pack on a bench to reserve a space upon his return from the bar.

It was the last lap of a disastrous journey for him. He had planned a holiday with his partner in the south of France. At the pension where they were staying, she had suddenly preferred – as if choosing a dress - a ginger-haired Irishman with a fine repertoire of songs and an infectious smile and left the pension with her new find without regret or apology. He had felt disposable and diminished. He then drove his ancient car back as far as Dijon, where it coughed its last. He had hardly enough credit in his account to pay for the bus journey home. Broke and love-lorn, he queued for his half a pint of beer.

Steering through the crowd and with his beer slopping over his wrist, he returned to his seat to find his pack on the floor, and a strikingly attractive young man stretched out on his seat, arms behind his head, smiling broadly.

'That's my seat. I put my pack there to reserve it. May I sit there, please?'

'Ha, what do we have here?' the man chuckled to an admiring circle of women sitting around him. 'A rule-bound bourgeois claiming his ill-gotten property rights?'

'I simply reserved a seat, that's all.'

'Ah, we make the rules, do we? The rest stand while His Highness gets his drink. Er..no. Not this time, duckie.'

'One last time, then. May I have my reserved seat, please?'

'Not a chance,' and with a mischievous and light-hearted glance, hands still behind his neck, he gently reclined onto the lap of a giggling girl sitting beside him, spreading his legs over Marcus's seat.

'Get out of my seat,' said Marcus quietly.

The man clicked his tongue regretfully and, still smiling good-naturedly, shook his head. His audience tinkled with approval.

For Marcus, the derisory click from the man's mouth burst open the furnace door letting out a roaring rage of retribution and revenge upon all who had demeaned and diminished him. In an instant, he dumped his self-guilt and self-disgust onto others who would pay for his misery. A voice from somewhere within him spoke quietly to the man.

'If you don't get out of my seat now, I will kill you.'

Still reclining on the lap of the girl, the man drawled,

'This anxious little fellow is clearly mad. However, I think it may be wise for us to reconvene elsewhere. Don't you think?

'He got up, smiled at Marcus, and the entourage pushed off into the crowd.

Marcus sat and nursed his half a pint of beer. He took a deep breath of relief. He realised what a dangerous situation he had landed himself in. Yes, threatening remarks threaten those who threaten. If that man had not got up from the seat, Marcus would have killed him, and the implications of a long prison sentence and indelible guilt would be a lifelong prospect. But, if the man had refused to give up his seat, and Marcus had not attempted to carry out his threat, his loss of face and self-worth would have been unendurable. Either way, it could have been a disaster.

Seething with contradictory thoughts, he sipped his beer, oblivious of the bar crowd. Then, he felt like getting a breath of fresh air, an escape from the immediate past, so he headed for the foredeck. It was dark and almost deserted by passengers. He rested his elbows on the railing and breathed the sweet air of relief deeply. Cool night air cleansed his mind, and he sighed with relief at his escape. Then he spotted the man, the same man, standing with his back to some railings, smiling at Marcus.

'Ah, our pet bourgeois pops up again. Very cool, I must say. But… really now. Would you, I mean really, have killed me?'

Marcus smiled. Second chance. Is now the moment?

Lust

Five of us men, mediocre, middle-aged and muddled, met in a pub every Saturday. I might have added maudlin and morose, but that would be taking it too far. Anyway, here, by the bar, we ruminated and rumbled about our ordinary and forgettable lives. Then, one day, one of our numbers brought something new into our meanderings, which started a stirring somewhere in the sump of my soul. He was a small and porky man, given a hopeful and heroic name by his parents - Nelson. Ludicrous and laughable, his drinking friends felt, though they kept those thoughts below their level of conscious contempt. He used to tap on the outside of our conversations like a small child wanting to be let in. Until, one day, he arrived at the pub definitely different. He appeared bright and breezy, waiting for the right moment to be let into our conversation.

'Hey, what is it, Nelson? You've been dying to tell us something all day. Go on, spit it out.'

This was not the entry with the flourish of trumpets he had wished for, but anyway, he pulled a small photograph from his pocket and passed it to us.

'Look, I've got something special to show you.'

We examined the photograph of rather an attractive young woman. Then he said with the smallest smirk.

'Furry, furry sucksie, eh, eh?'

'What did you say? Didn't catch that.'

'You know, sucksie, don't you think? She's my girlfriend.'

His little pink tongue flicked out from his lips. I turned away. I did not want to go where my subconscious was leading me.

Then I saw it, that moment at a pub with mates, a pinhole to peer through into the twilight of delusion of another, without the prospect of admission and self-torture. Was there lust lurking in Nelson? Could I see a lusty, raunchy, rude and reckless, immoderate and immediate Nelson? No? Or was it lust that, in his dull and distant soul, was lit with a lesser flame, flickering and feeble, far from that of a furious and victorious male? Or did I see in his mind's eye a distant and illusory light at the far end of a dark and lonely tunnel? Lust, love, dreams of the end of solitude? Whatever.

We colluded, had a pint or two and split up mid-afternoon as usual.

A month later, the rest of us had drunk our first pint when Nelson turned up – with a companion. A tall brown-eyed woman with a smile so natural and open-hearted that it silenced the small talk of us men. She treated us as normal, socially competent people who might well have something of interest or humour to share. We tried our best and gazed furtively into a fresh new world. After an hour, they left.

And they never came back.

Sin

Luscious, lascivious, and delicious,

Unlawful, immoral, wicked and wrong?

Depends who knows best, who feels least,

Who gets the voice to sing the song.

Smack your lips, and swallow the feast,

Stare down gluttony, banish the beast.

Gulp with contrition, gag at the thought.

Then, there's wrath, blood boiling and blind,

Enraged soul to set others to nought,

Fermenting obsession, crushing the mind.

Pride denies others' virtue with withering thought.

Upon others' riches, greed breeds designs, covetous and sly.

While sloth shuffles slowly through duty and debt.

But all sins grin into the sinner's eye.

Pay the wages of sin with conscience and set

Contrition a chance to free one's life.

But sin, the word so sharp and thin

Slices through self-delusion like a knife.

"Repent in this world", it beckons, "and win".

Shame and regret you should feel in this life

But pretend that sin never was, stokes God's ire.

And your burning soul will roast in hell's fire.

Pride precedes

Skiing down the piste of life, all fancy-free
Who'd have thought a fall would quietly wait?
Who'd have thought it might be me?
Who'd have thought it'd be my fate?

It's free will, luck and being clever
Without a worry nor a care
As the present whizzes by forever
Until that point, until you're there.

Of course, I'm from the privileged few,
Who expects to stay in the prime of life
Where nothing's stale, and all is new.
No need for guilt, no need for strife.

It's natural I'm white and bright.
I'm male, too; I have it all, let's be blunt.
Not Pee See, I know, so keep it out of sight.
Just elbow past rivals and keep out in front.

Perhaps a passing thought for those who plod
Across dreary plains to who knows where,
Towards their end and their distant god,
Without respite, love, or care.

The snow glows golden on the lower slopes,

I sweep confident!!......

42

Scorpion

The first time, a smooth stone upturned
Revealed a scorpion attacking now
Venomous sting arched over its back.
Poised to puncture, primed to poison.
Fright blinds first sight in violent recoil,
But burns deep in memory.
Slam the stone, squash the scorpion.
Flee the present, live another day.

The second time is happenstance.
Another scorpion under a stone
This time, two young daughters spot it.
Whooping with surprise, "it's clicking.
It's ticking. Has it got a clock inside?"
"It's dancing, see! One back, two forward.
It's doing the cha cha cha."
Father only remembers it with them.
And now scorpions caper in dad's mind,
They sing and sting, prance and lance.
Timelessly twitching in his mind.

Losing the Place

Sleep rough and dark is not only outside,

It lurks inside us too, and no one knows where.

Dangerous, deadly perhaps, but night hides all.

Frost finds travellers without a roof,

Chills dream of a warmer world,

Freezes their will to wander in tundra wastes.

Cancels time to rise, cramps the limbs,

Gropes, grips, beckons to the half-dead.

Rain, sweet for those with roofs above their heads,

Spatters windowpanes, reminding how dry they are inside.

For those without, rain falls cold on sodden clothes.

No networks of love, protection and laughter here,

But random spikes of hate, grimace and disgust.

Kicking a body huddled in an alley - for fun.

But sneering jeers at least don't draw blood.

Escape from now for the faintest flash of comfort.

Turn back and remember home, where warmth is shared.

To belong, laugh and grow, create a place together.

This, this is home. To leave it and walk away.

Is to lose it, to cut adrift and roam a placeless world

The Price of Gold

The locomotive heaved to a halt, expressed the last pant of steam and stood facing the buffers at the end of the line. Sand whispered over the tracks and licked a decrepit wooden platform and a huddle of nearby huts. No frenzy of passengers, no cries of porters, no bustle of travel, just a few refugees from the sun, hiding in rare spots of shade. We five students were also spending the night at this desolate spot in the desert to be sure of catching the train to Quetta the next morning. There was only one train a week. It was on Thursdays. This was not going to be a safe place to sleep, as we quickly realised, having unloaded our rucksacks from the taxi. We kept a watch during the night. Shadows and suspicious noises kept us awake until dawn.

Early next morning, before breathless heat desiccated any dream of cool and comfort, a swarm of vans and jeeps approached the railway station, each vehicle spewing a cloud of dust into the faces of those following. Soon, the railway carriages were surrounded by men, grim, bearded, in dark green kaftans, heaving enormous bundles of luggage into the railway carriages. Three men prowled in dark glasses – a disguise as well as a badge of menace - watchful, seeing all. Very dangerous. One stopped for an instant and maybe glanced in our direction. The slightest reaction would imply guilt and the threat of retribution.

We quickly boarded the train to secure seats and find a half-empty third-class compartment. Others were not far behind and, to our consternation, peered into the carriage through the window, spotted the presence of European travellers, and piled in. Soon, our compartment was packed to the point of suffocation. Some hours passed, police and customs officials came in trucks with armed soldiers and moved from carriage to carriage to hold an inspection of luggage. Of course, it was impractical to carry out a search when luggage was stacked to the ceiling and could not be inspected without all of it first being removed from the carriage. The customs officials summoned one of the passengers outside for a short interchange, and he returned after a few moments with a face set in anger. A number of other passengers were detained and stood dejectedly in the direct sun, awaiting an uncertain fate.

After a stifling two hours, the train lurched backwards for a few minutes, and the carriages were left in the sun while the engine looped round to the front. Then, with a triumphant whistle, the journey began. After four hours, the train stopped. The Iran-Pakistan frontier. A few huts were the only sign of human habitation. Immediately we could see a line of passengers with the same unmanageable luggage trying to make it to the train. Six men on horseback wielding swords appeared in the dust from the opposite direction. They swooped down on the shambling line. There was a moment when we could witness harsh cries, slaughter, and blood on the sand. But we could see the horsemen were beating the men with the flat of their swords. A few in the line were finally able to make it to the train with their luggage and attempted to board, while others abandoned theirs in the sand and scampered to the train. There was more upheaval while the new refugee passengers tried to secure entry into compartments packed solid to the roof. The horsemen wheel porters appeared from the haze and carried off the abandoned piles of luggage. The train signalled the end of the scene with a steamy whistle and proceeded slowly east.

But it had only been an hour when the wind started to roar like an enraged dragon. Nothing could be seen except dust, closed windows, airless carriages. The train stopped, men jumped down from the carriages to inspect the disappearance of the rail tracks. There was sand everywhere, and we seemed abandoned in an endless impassable desert. After some time, men with shovels spent three hours clearing the tracks, and the train crept forward a hundred meters at a time. As we climbed back into the carriage, we spotted a small notice in faded English on the carriage interior. It said, "Do not get out of the train to pick flowers."

Leaving the sandy desert, the train started to climb, doggedly puffing through gorges, up steep inclines, more bare rock and less sand. The train stopped at the first station of a town eight hours later. Suddenly the carriages were heaving with disembarking passengers, throwing their luggage onto the platform or the ground, swearing, barging, and pushing. The same men with dark glasses quietly watched them. Then we noticed six other men dressed differently. Afghan? Not from Iran anyway. They surround the passengers with their luggage. Other men similarly dressed stood behind them. All of them were wearing unfamiliar headwear, the pakhul, with traditional Afghan clothing. All other passengers, travellers, porters melted away. We pulled back from the window. Something was about to happen. But confrontation there was none, merely a transaction between parties that distrusted each other and one involving a commodity of great value, judging by the threat of potential violence. The luggage was taken away in lorries parked outside the station. The carriages were nearly empty, there was air to breathe, and the remaining passengers started to chat. The train started for its last stretch to Quetta. As it left the station, one of us exclaimed, 'Hey, I've actually seen a woman - the first in four days.' We laughed and felt ashamed.

Platform Talk

"Adrian! There you are. I was wondering if you'd muddled the train time. It wouldn't be the first time, though..."

"No, my darling, nor it would. But you did ask me especially to be here. You know, for a fond farewell and... maybe something else, I think, from the expression on your face."

"Well, there is something….."

"Yeah, I know. Look, whatever it is, it's bound to be difficult. I'm away for eight weeks, and things haven't been all that smooth between us lately, have they? You know - the cliffs of Dover and all that. So, yeah, let's talk."

"Yes, Adrian. But we better hurry up about it. People are slamming carriage doors, and the guard seems serious. Look..."

"OMG, here comes James. I think you've met him. He's the guy I'm going to teach with. I've told you about him."

"Hey, Adrian... and Helen! Good to see you. Great! So, Helen, are you coming over to the States to visit us, then? Why not? Cheap trans-Atlantic flight and you could…."

"James, look, Adrian and I have something to discuss before you guys leave. Do you think you could give us a few minutes alone?"

"Yeah, okay, no prob. Jesus, that's the whistle. The train is leaving. You'd better hop on. Come on, NOW!"

And did Adrian wave from the carriage window? No, he did not. I was left on Platform 6, Paddington Station. Alone. He left without the news I had planned to share with him and also left me alone with the pivot of my life, my unborn child - but not our unborn child. Adrian had left without that knowledge. Why had I planned to tell him then before he left for eight weeks? I could have waited until he got back. Answer? Insecurity. He had become strangely distant recently, preoccupied, vague, intermittently deaf. Oh yes, I could read those signs. To tell him I was pregnant before he left - was it to trap him? Shame him into staying with me? Anyway, that was a high-risk strategy. If that was my motive, telling him the news would have brought shame on myself and the whole relationship. And also, he might take one fleeting look at this future and flee. And….. not to tell? It was unfair on both of us – and on the baby. Adrian should know. After all, he may be delighted, I thought, even if he does not want to live with me - stuck!

So what did I do? I waited eight weeks and told him the day he got back from the USA.

"How sure are you it is mine?" A clear conscience and a clear answer were enough to dispel doubt. "So, do you want to live with me?" I remember how he asked me that as if he was asking if I wanted a second slice of toast.

"Yes," I replied.

"Okay," he said with a shrug, maybe with the faintest of smiles. It was an anticlimax at a moment that surely cried out for love, romance and excitement. So it was a compromise, a listless beginning of our life together. Now, after twelve years with Arabella sitting at the table engrossed in her homework, can I believe myself when I say, "Actually, we both recovered, made the best of our shaky ambivalent beginning and live… well, quite a happy life together. Paddington Station was a shared history, an interesting memory that can be recalled by either of us without too much regret."

Moving On

Zanda wriggles his scales on a smooth flat rock,

Lazily puffs smoke into the evening sun.

Flicking his tail with a clatter, Zanda feels bored.

Emperor of all the valleys and mountains,

Seizing sheep in horny grip, biting bulls by the neck.

The scourge of all creatures living in the land.

Living's easy, but living's lonely, living's sad.

Zanda sees far off a young woman on a donkey,

Coming fearlessly towards the Emperor dragon.

"She'd make a tasty morsel; let us wait and see."

She stops and catches his hooded eye with hers.

She smiles.

"So, what would a young maiden want with me then?"

"I am Faridha; I am the Sultan's daughter.

I propose a test of strength with you, Zanda."

A growl of amusement, a leer of yellow fangs.

'And if you should looooose, little one, what then?"

As Zanda's tail curls around Faridha's back.

"Eat me, of course, what else? But if it's me that wins,

You must fly away, leave this valley forever."

"I accept little one. So, what is this contest?"

"You must crush a rock so hard; it gives out milk."

"Ha!" scoffs Zanda gripping a boulder with his teeth.

A splitting cracking noise of crumbling rock,

And he lets fall a pile of gravel from his jaws.

"There, little one. Now let us see what you can do."

"Ah, Zanda, can't you see? No milk, only gravel."

Zanda narrows his hooded eyes and hisses.

Faridha takes a large round stone, flat and pale

From her donkey's saddle and squeezes it hard

Until milk flows fast and free between her fingers.

Zanda roars with rage, thinks a quick snap of fangs

Might bite off humiliation, and no one would know.

But Zanda, as many emperors before him, is bored.

New tastes, new vistas, new life - all lie elsewhere.

He roars and, with a smirk, flies off.

Faridha waits until Zanda has flown from sight,

Then recovers the squashed round cheese from the rock.

Mole

Mole earned his nickname by his sleek, smooth hair that lay flat along with his head and neck. He was small for his age and, at six years old, was at least a hand's breadth shorter than me. He talked in a tight chuckle, his teeth reluctant to let words out of his mouth. He ran in a lopsided canter, laughing as he sped ahead of me. I was allowed to play with him once a week, and my mother used to drive a couple of miles to the edge of the wood where Mole and his mother lived. Thinking back on those times, I realise Mrs Hopkins was a distressed member of the gentry, living a precarious and impoverished existence as a widow. She and my mother used to "take lunch", as they called it, at Mrs Hopkins's house - bread and margarine with homemade jam on a rickety old table outside her house, which hardly earned that phrase they both used without a hint of irony.

As soon as the parents waved us away with, "Off you go and play. But don't go too far, will you now," Mole and I fled far, very far, and wide into the wood. He showed me dragonflies, glittering and clattering over the pond, ants seething under tree stumps, and beetles busy and black in the bracken. But there was one creature that he was constantly talking about - Wopsie. He lived in a burrow under an ancient oak tree. Mole and Wopsie had long conversations about life in the forest, about being wild and living on the edge of a wood and "on the edge of... people," as Mole would put it. "He knows things, and he tells me. I bring him nuts and food, and it's all gone the next day. Every time. We talk about how we can live together away from mum and all the others and be happy, just us in the wood."

I never did get to see Wopsie. Although, through Mole, I became familiar with a maze of confusing and astonishing facts about wilderness, which Wopsie used to tell him. Squirrels fly at night and only pretend they can't during the day. When there is a full moon, a man with fur trousers and no shirt on comes and plays a sort of flute and keeps on laughing. Moles, "like meeee!" shouts Mole, grinning, build cities under the ground, but not like we do. They build them by digging the soil away, leaving the houses on either side.

Then something happened that changed everything. One day, Mole and I returned from the wood and thought we would steal up to Mrs Hopkins and my mother as they were having lunch. Crouching behind a low wall, we both quite clearly heard Mrs Hopkins say, "Well, you know Mike is a little... backward, you know, and I have to send him to a special school. Now he's six, well, nearly seven now. It'll be good for him to have other children around. Of course, I'll have to move into town to be close to the school."

Mother clucked sympathy and replied, "Mike is a lovely little boy – a credit to you, of course. But he is a little strange, and being with other children will teach him how... to be in company." Mole heard every word from behind the wall. He seemed to shrink and become even more mole-like. A long silence and then, "I have to tell Wopsie. Let's go."

We creep away and race to Wopsie's burrow. The food we had left is still there. We wait, and Mole calls Wopsie, quietly at first and then louder until he is shouting at the entrance of Wopsie's burrow. But there's absolute silence, no reply. "He's gone. GONE," Mole starts wailing, "He's gone, he's gone," pressing his forehead into the hole.

An Unintended Pilgrimage

There is a cave high in the Himalayas far above the noisome city and dusty plain, where Shiva told secrets of immortality, where his lingam of ice waxes and wanes with the coming and going of the seasons. For a month, the snows melt enough for pilgrims to witness them. Sixty thousand pilgrims toil in a line stitched against the snow. There is a back route to the cave, precipitous and dangerous, as are all shortcuts to divine knowledge. Two frivolous foreigners decide to take that route. All they sought was adventure, hardly immortal truths at all. The path starts no more than a ragged notch along a precipitous stony slope, falling away to a gnashing glacial torrent far below. One false step would not kill in free fall but in bone snapping bounces. The path must cross the gorge on an ice bridge and within a small blue tunnel of melting water, suffused with the roar of the torrent far below. Six hours of further dangerous walking takes them to the next ice bridge, where the path must cross to the other side. But the ice bridge has melted. Night rises from the gorge beneath. The two travellers lie down to sleep on the only level space available. They stare at the stars above and hear the roar of their fate below. They hold hands and say goodbye. As dawn breaks meanly in the shadows, they leave, perhaps to witness the death of the other. For every footfall, a single mistake means goodbye. But after seven hours, they take the last step to safety. A glance, a sigh of relief, of joy, of reprieve. They, too, had been on a pilgrimage after all.

Baggy Clopper

Shafts of sunlight like chords of music slant through the canopy of trees far above. Birds chortle deep purple in the shadows. Chirrups, rustlings and calls sever the silence. In the penumbra, a path leads away into the deepest gloom, and on it, a man walks slowly. He is old, he is white - an exotic fauna in the tropical forest, and he is weeping. Tears course down his face, but he does not seem to be grieving nor tottering abroad in strange and dangerous places, unaware of other eyes which have long been watching him. He moves slowly like a fish in an aquarium. He says quietly to himself over and over again as if reciting a prayer, 'It's not true, it's not true. I didn't do these things. I didn't save them; I never touched the girl. I didn't. I didn't. How could they think this? Yet, he is sighing and smiling and looks up at the trees from time to time, as if searching for relief and rest there. Later along the path, he chants, '…….I am all right now. I am okay. I am okay. I don't know why, but I am, I am.'

He had a miserable war in Burma. A private, always a private, pasty, pimply, small, with skin soft like an under-inflated balloon, he had been encumbered with a nickname which had pursued him from the Fens of Eastern England to the jungles of South-east Asia. Baggy Clopper. In the barracks in India before going to the front line, he had attracted the jeers and butts of other insecure but-if-it-came-to-a-fight-confident squaddies. Hot chillies secreted in his stew, dead lizards hidden in his bunk, watchful eyes and sneering mouths, always ready to spill contempt. He was never safe in his solitude.

They were overrun by the Japanese, often on bicycles, well trained, stoical and far, far too good. As he walks through the forest, he remembers in the war now only its silence, empty of sound, as if all creatures were holding their breath until a chatter of machine-gun fire and short, clipped orders from the enemy who instantly withdrew into the shadows, leaving his companions gurgling bright red onto the green leaves of the forest floor. He stops to muse on how the forest seemed so silent unlike as he remembered it.

The Japanese had overrun the British lines breaking them up into small bands of soldiers, dis-spirited and lost. He had fled, stub-toed, panicked, reeling through the forest with a taste of rust and old blood and had arrived at the edge of the forest and stumbled upon a small village of thatched bamboo buildings. He had left others behind for dead, become totally lost, then thirsty. Bitten by insects so that his eyes were almost closed, he waited behind a tree. After all the extreme violence and danger, and with possible salvation in his sight, he was seized with shyness. How could he show himself in such a pitiable state, dirty, discoloured and misshapen? Events cut short his hesitation as he was spotted as he shambled out into the open ground. Women and children scattered at the arrival of one pathetic, unravelled soldier. A band of villagers and, it turned out, the headman converged on him. With a few words of the headman's in English, Baggy was able to persuade them of his nationality and was surprised at the warmth of his reception – reasons for which he learnt later. The headman told him about the arrival of Japanese soldiers who had crucified three men in an attempt to find out the sources of information that had enabled the British to ambush a Japanese convoy. They were reluctant to allow him to stay but, after hours of discussion, relented and provided a small hut at the edge of the village and for an emergency, a hiding hole under it stuffed full of bamboo poles and seething with snakes and rats.

Over the next eight months, he became a working guest, fixing iron tools and working in the fields. An old woman was allocated to look after him. She was almost toothless, laughed a great deal, throwing her head back from the sack-like hse which she wore. She laughed at Baggy's few words of the local language, either because she did not understand them or maybe because she did. Baggy was seldom sure. However, for him, laughter was like soft rain after a drought of a lifetime. Now it nurtured him, and he wept to hear it. She had a daughter who lived behind the hut, and it was she who gave him his most enduring memory of that time. It was her smile he remembered, so fleeting and transforming, that when it faded, all who saw it longed to see it again. She seldom spoke and, in repose, had an expression of permanent sadness. Her smile was so sudden and celebratory that all tried to induce her to smile and help her escape her indelible sadness, even if merely for a moment. Few managed to do so, and Baggy, so effortlessly successful with her mother, least of all, but he managed to do so attempting his few words of the Karen language on about three occasions. Other than those beatific moments, he had no other sign of recognition nor contact of any sort with her during his eight-month stay.

The dry season marched through glaring skies and full sun. Baggy worked in the paddy fields, knee-deep in red mud, humming along to the Karen songs, rounds sung in teasing competition between men and women. Bent double, they all transplanted bright green seedlings into shallow trays of brown water. Over the next few weeks, the monsoon gradually puffed itself up into massive clouds lit gold and bruised purple every evening. Then, one day, not the usual thunder and lightning of the afternoon, but the real monsoon arrived, bringing along the rains with a silver hush, every day, all day. Squalls of wind drove brown-red wavelets across flooded fields dotted with green sparks. It was back-breaking work with lean rations, but at least, it was living in a space free of World War and for Baggy, free of contempt. Everyone was aware of the reprieve and celebrated it with cautious expressions of gratitude. Long, may it last, but how could it?

Three months went by, the rains receded, the dry land crops of maise and millet were planted, houses repaired, and then the harvesting of the paddy crop started. Large gangs of men and women swarmed over one field at a time, cutting the golden paddy stalks with sickles, stacking, carrying them back to the village, winnowing and drying the grain on mats. It was a fourteen-hour day for all except children and the oldest, who cooked meals and brought them to the fields. He had no time for introspection and just enough physical energy to cope with a relentless work rate. All relied on each other at this time, and dropping out without obvious reason, meant irretrievable loss of reputation. Baggy coped.

One evening shortly after the festival, families were sitting outside their houses on bamboo mats talking, but there stood in the shadow of the wood, motionless, two Japanese soldiers. Watching. One cry of alarm, others looked up from sewing, winnowing, smoking pipes, and suddenly all the village was on its feet and struck silent. The soldiers marched into the clearing in the centre of the houses. Baggy slipped round the back of his hut and forced himself into a dark corner, then rammed himself into the bamboo store, end-on to the shafts and into the shadows where snakes lie. He cowered. And waited. Boots appeared in the slit of outside vision, stopped, a short-order given, given again in anger at the end of a bayonet, and Baggy's escape was over. He was marched off in front of the two soldiers. At the point of leaving the village, one of the soldiers turned around and, in a verbal explosion like iron filings, shouted a message of what everyone understood as a sentence of retribution.

"We know you sheltered an enemy. We will be back, and we will exact from you the price we want."

Maybe this was the message, maybe not. No one spoke Japanese, but all knew it served a sentence of death for many of those who remained in the village.

The three ran through the forest with Baggy between the two soldiers. Then he heard gunfire nearby and, through the sweat and terror, felt the war somehow had taken a different turn. The soldiers were nervous brittle, argued between themselves and kept changing their minds over the route through the forest. After two hours of running, stopping and listening, they arrived at a small encampment. He was thrown into a barbed wire cage, kicked twice and left to cough and gasp in the mud under the trees. Soldiers were breaking camp hurriedly and preparing to leave. Then, the noise of more small arms fires nearby echoed through the forest. The officer came out of his tent and marched up to the barbed wire. Baggy knew what was going to happen and waited for his death. The officer waited too and smiled at him through the barbed wire. He reached for his revolver very slowly, and later Baggy remembered that the officer sighed as he slid the safety catch off and raised his weapon. A fusillade of fire shattered everything. The officer ran back to the tent but was cut down by machine gunfire. Baggy was rescued by Australian soldiers, tough, laconic, and kind. The next few months were a blur of illnesses, including malaria, and troops returning to the front line, spilling piles of equipment, shouting orders at railway stations and port embarkations, through holding camps and then a troopship home.

The first time he was able to reflect on the past year was in the shed at his allotment as he sat in the evening sun. Here he was home in the Fens, living with his mother again, back to her dentures, her demands, her piles of magazines in the bedrooms and down the stairs, and out into the hall. Slowly, he realised the sadness of his life, which had been thrown into relief by his stay with the Karen people. There had been physical hardship and fear of death, but no contempt, no bullying, no sense of stasis and regret over the emptiness of the past. That escape had enabled him to see that redemption might be possible. Otherwise, if he did not find it, he would die. What could he call his own? What had he done, which he was proud of? What had he created? When had he ever gone so far as to brush lips with someone who might have loved him? He knew the future offered no chance for new accomplishments, so it was in the past that redemption must be found for the future. From that moment, he decided to

return to the Karen village where he had spent eight months of the war. His savings would provide funds to buy the airfare. He would do it.

So, it was on an April day, seventeen years later, that he arrived at the village with a young student interpreter he had picked up at the local airport. They got down from the bus, and Baggy vaguely recognised the village, and he simply did not have a plan. He hoped that maybe he would see his friends again (he realised that it was the first time he wanted to call anyone that). They might even welcome him. Maybe, the daughter would light up his life with her smile just once more. Maybe, he could stay there and disappear from the Fens of England forever, where the smell of his mother's stale cigarette smoke pursued him everywhere, and he was the butt of three strapping, jeering, beer-drinking brothers. Maybe he would work in the fields again and be a recognised and useful member of the community.

He stood in the centre of the village, becoming increasingly confused. Then, there was a shout from an old woman, who got up from her bamboo mat in front of her house, rushed to him, laughing and said something he did not understand. The village headman came but was a much younger man than the headman Baggy had known. Soon, he was surrounded by villagers, who, he slowly realised, seemed excited and delighted by him. How could this be? Finally, the present headman's father and a number of others

whom he half-recognised escorted him with great cordiality to the headman's house. The headman gave an impromptu speech to a small crowd, for which the student murmured a shortened translation to Baggy. The gist was that everyone was honoured and delighted that the hero had returned. They had all wanted to thank him and celebrate his heroic acts but had given up hope that he would ever return. Now, both his bravery - and something else at which the student laughed in an embarrassed way and for the time being failed to translate - had become a legend and were told as stories to the children in the evening.

Baggy asked the interpreter what he was supposed to have done. 'But you saved us from the Japanese soldiers. They took you away, said they would come back and kill some more of us. You were tortured but resisted and, when the Australians came, you sent them to our village to protect us. We owe you our lives. Now you have returned, we will honour you'. He started to say that all this was not true, but his interpreter said that any denial would spoil a joyful reunion. Then, from the back of the crowd, a young man in his mid-teens and behind him an older woman approached Baggy. The village headman took his elbow gently and said softly, "This is your son – welcome him." The young man was very handsome and clearly half-Karen and a half-European. Two steps behind him stood his mother as if she was presenting him to Baggy. He recognised her at exactly

the same time as she smiled, so briefly and completely that it lit the world for him one last time. He started to explain to his interpreter that he had hardly talked to her during his stay at her mother's house, let alone touch her, but then stopped when he realised the embarrassment his denial might cause her. He cried out and stumbled forward to embrace the young man. People laughed indulgently and then gradually dispersed in a quiet and tactful manner except for a small group of senior men who invited him for an evening meal. He mumbled an apology and said he needed to be by himself. He wandered out of the village towards the forest. The first green shadows of outlying trees, the clear bell-like ringing of the cicadas, and then the sweet-scented foliage of the forest enveloped him.

The Cracking Plains

A desert eagle soaring high above the cracking plains of Sudan might see a plume of white dust far below. It billows from a small speck as it moves across a desiccated and dusty wilderness and hangs in the air for a few minutes before dissipating. That speck is a Land Cruiser carrying a polyglot crew on an important Mission (note the capital letter, please). We are experts acting for an international bank on the way to evaluate a large irrigation scheme, which it had financed. In the minibus are two Swedes, taciturn, serious and giving the impression of always knowing better without giving any evidence that this was the case. There is also an unsettlingly intelligent Keralan economist whose Malayalam-inflected English defies all intelligible limits of phonetic speed. Finally, a large Texan sits at the back, and his drawl is so drawn out and so bored that it dribbles down his chin. The driver is a genial Sudanese, whose name is "Jim". No women with us, no diversity of heart, vision or expression, no relief for anyone of us. So, here we are, stuck with each other in a wagon wedged to the edge on a journey across an everlasting plain.

Escape from our mobile prison might be expected to invite a keen interest in the landscape and people we meet outside, but an ever-receding flat horizon does not encourage it. Every few hours, a huge truck passes, swirling dust in its

wake. Occasionally, a bent tree, solitary and forlorn, punctuates the same distant line. Ocean voyages under sail must have seemed like this – the bustle of setting sail, chasing an unchanging flat line for weeks. Here, ports of call are transport cafes. Massive muscle-bound trucks park haphazardly around small huts from which tiny drivers jump down and hurry to the café for bean stews, flatbread, fried goat meat and tea. The talk over steaming plates is fast and concentrated – the state of the road, reports of hijackers at night, what the army is doing, smuggling. Not a woman in sight. Then we would leave the café, struck by a breath-taking stroke of heat and have to swim through a shimmering gap between the fan-cooled cafe and air-conditioned car. Never is the return to our prison so welcome.

On and on for another five hours across the cracking plain. Then I see it. A small flat hill, a table of golden sandstone visible on the horizon - the first sighting of land in a limitless ocean. Then another, bigger than the first, perhaps half a kilometre long and eighty meters high, then another until we are surrounded by an archipelago of table topped hills, and our track weaves between them. Now there is movement in the landscape, and the long thin line between emptiness and more emptiness is broken. I see two women carrying firewood on their backs – my first for some days.

"Look!" shouts the driver, a gold tooth shining in his black beard. He turns to me as I sit in the front seat. "Look!"

and he laughs. Through the windscreen, I see a range of mountains in the evening sun. Monotony had become a habit. Nothing to see, and you see nothing – even mountains on the edge of the world. My eyes roll upwards and upwards. There they are, misty blue as grape bloom, promising cool shadows and fresh air. Ethiopia! The driver stops the Land Cruiser, and we tumble out. I forget if anyone said anything. Suddenly the repose of mountains is rented by a scream of low-flying warplanes. Of course, I remember. Ethiopia is at war with Eritrea. We climb back into the car and wait for the driver to take us to the irrigation scheme. No one speaks.

Then, there is the return journey.

Remembering

Memory is a guest; memory is a ghost
Appears and stays, haunts and goes,
Flicking familiar, unbidden and sweet
Or gurgling ugly from a past best lost.

Small boy alone at school
Hare lip, face stitched together
No hiding place, no forgiving smile.
School kids, point, smirk and jibe.
"Lippy", "cut face", "scarlip".
Splintered glass is buried still.
Under the beard, he grows now.

One day he strides the streets,
Bearded, suited, the man about town.
He spots a man shuffling by
Who gives him a knowing smile of familiar shape,
Who knows what lies beneath his beard.

Regeneration

Stone eyes stare through green leaves.

And blink when no one is there.

Tilted torsos of forgotten gods

Slowly subside from sight.

Marble steps, cracked and worn.

Lack the warmth of worshippers' feet.

Temple walls gripped by creepers.

Crack, crumble, twist and turn.

Embraced in place by their destroyer.

Roots of ancient trees flow over.

Foundations long lost to memory.

Now birds chirrup where priests chanted,

And stealthy four-footed creatures stalk.

Where pilgrims shuffled to confession,

Snakes coil around branches waiting for prey.

Where people once talked to gods, the forest resumes.

Very Late Cretaceous

You will only know me by my bones.

Buried deep in slabs of rock in far off time.

I lived when forests were full and the grass was lush.

We munched leaves of luscious trees.

We grew so tall we reached the highest fruit.

We grew so huge we rested in water to float our weight.

We slumbered and lumbered through an age of plenty.

Shadows slowly crept up on our kind.

We lay eggs and guard them until they hatch.

We are not cold-blooded in metaphor nor in life,

We have to warm ourselves in the morning sun.

So, it was at night that they came for us.

Little creatures with skins of brownish fur.

They came squeaking, skittering between our legs.

They ate our eggs, grew larger, started to take our young.

Then, there was the day when the earth shook.

One long shudder like none had ever felt before,

A moment's silence, then shrieking terror.

Flying reptiles burst upwards in fright,

Iguanas stampede and all stop chewing.

All know their world was on edge.

Red glow at night and ash plumes filled the sky.

The sun was shrouded for years and years.

All was cold, cold, cold.

Grasses died, trees failed, flowers shrivelled.

We starved and traipsed the plains for green.

We plodded in dark, dust and drought

Until some started to die.

Now, hear this, you furless, new age monkeys.

Can't you learn from what happened to us?

How will you be understood when you are gone?

Because you too are going to go and very soon.

Never-Ending Dance

Catherine wheel whizzing, fizzing circles of light,

Green, purple, showering sparks of gold.

Then, the dervish dance done goes dead in the night.

Smiling faces turn to the new, blank out the old.

You, Catherine, sparkled for me long ago,

Your eyes on mine, ready to take the chance.

Why do I compare you to a firework show?

Because you dazzled me, led me to an endless dance.

I did not know your firework was for all to see,

Dancing, teasing, disguising your despair.

Your show went on and on - not just for me.

Breathless, hectic, we half knew but never gave a care.

Suddenly, you were gone, snuffed out, energy spent.

Light programmed to go out, and out you went.

Worm

Shall I tell you a story that may change your life, maybe for the worse? I think it will. You, the reader, also have a choice. Of course, you do. So, make that choice and lend an ear.

I am a shaman. I am from the jungles of India. I deal in magic, sorcery and witchcraft with maharajas in marble halls, as I do with the wild and mad of the forest. For some, I cast out evil godlings and mischief-makers in the Great Wheel of Life. But for some, I put them back in. I, for favours and other considerations, wreak revenge upon others, and for this purpose, I use the Prabhu worm. It is a tiny maggot, no bigger than a grain of rice.

The victim identified by my masters is persuaded to chat with my victim, affably and confidently. I lower my voice and whisper conspiratorially in his ear. It is then I blow the Prabhu worm into his ear, and it starts its long journey, narrowing into his inner ear and into his brain. He suffers terrible headaches, loses his balance, beats his head against a stone and wishes he was dead. He loses his mind as the maggot burrows ever deeper into the soft tissues of the brain. For knowing onlookers, revenge can be enjoyed, relaxed and slow. There is plenty of time.

Now I am old, and it is difficult to find the Prabhu worm. These days few wish to inflict so slow a death. Instead, they

corrupt police. They shoot and depart to feast upon brighter and quicker achieved ends. Hah, now you have inclined your mind's ear to my story. Poof… you are already infected. You have the idea that the worm within you drive you mad. I depart. My story is over, my purpose fulfilled.

Laughter

We stole through a deep forest in central Africa with a mission that seemed increasingly absurd. It was to find out why monkeys were being exterminated and how to conserve their numbers. They were part of the local people's diet, were being shot with illegal guns and ammunition, and hence there was a potential threat of their extinction. As the evening deepened shadows, it became essential to find a safe place to sleep. Eventually, as darkness rose to the treetops, we saw some lights coming from a small village amongst the trees. We arrived at a circle of wooden huts, crouched in a forest clearing with a number of fires and cauldrons of food being cooked. After finding shelter, we were directed to one of the cooking hearths for a meal. By the fire, there stood a magnificent woman wafting a welcoming hand to the fire and steaming cauldron. She was at least six feet tall and magnificent, her movements magisterial. Yes, we thought and sat on the wooden bench by the cauldron. She served her stew with a ladle the size of a shovel. Gobbets of meat and vegetable submerged in a thick, rich sauce were slopped onto their aluminium plates. As we ate, she chatted in French, and it became clear that she had received a good education. But it was her humour, lit by the flash of her brilliant teeth that kept us happy and chuckling throughout our meal. Then, she asked us what we were doing so far from the city and our distant homes. We told her about our concern about the threat of extinction of monkeys through shooting and the illegal supply of firearms and ammunition.

It was the unexpected explosion of her laughter that we would always remember. Here were two earnest whites concerned about the extermination of monkeys, one of which they had just eaten. We immediately tuned our ears to the slightest tone of derision in her laughter. Was she laughing at us or with us? We could tell immediately. We started to laugh too.